Ancient Egypt

Rosie McCormick

Copyright © 2019 Core Knowledge Foundation
www.coreknowledge.org

All Rights Reserved.

Core Knowledge®, Core Knowledge Curriculum Series™,
Core Knowledge History and Geography™, and CKHG™
are trademarks of the Core Knowledge Foundation.

Trademarks and trade names are shown in this book
strictly for illustrative and educational purposes and are
the property of their respective owners. References herein
should not be regarded as affecting the validity of said
trademarks and trade names.

Printed in Canada

ISBN: 978-1-68380-394-2

Ancient Egypt

Table of Contents

Chapter 1	**The Nile River**	2
Chapter 2	**Pharaohs and Everyday People**	5
Chapter 3	**Pyramids and Mummies**	8
Chapter 4	**Gods and Goddesses**	13
Chapter 5	**Egyptian Writing**	16
Chapter 6	**Tutankhamen**	19
Chapter 7	**Hatshepsut**	23

CHAPTER 1

The Nile River

Long, long ago in ancient Egypt, the Nile River rose up above its banks and flooded the land. This happened each year. Farmers used the rich soil the river left behind to grow plants that could be eaten as food. The Nile River also brought water to the plants that grew.

To grow plants, Egyptian farmers first dug up the soil. Sometimes they used a hoe for digging. Then they dropped seeds into the ground. Animals such as cows stepped on the seeds and pushed them into the ground so that they would grow.

Sometimes farmers used a plow instead of a hoe to dig up the soil. Often an ox pulled the plow along.

Ancient Egypt was a civilization on the continent of Africa. The land of ancient Egypt lay along the Nile River. All around this land was a desert, called the Sahara Desert. Ancient Egypt became known as the gift of the Nile.

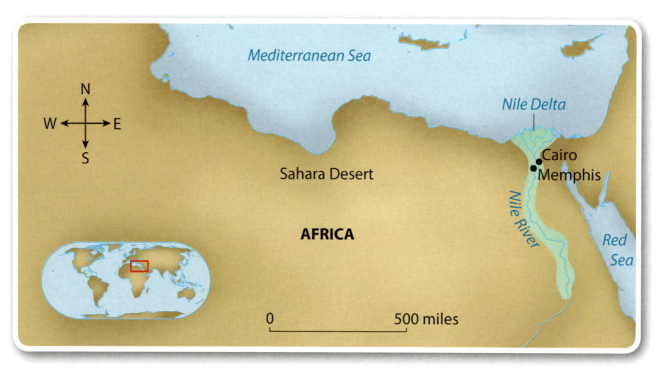

The Nile River is in northern Africa. It is more than four thousand miles long. The Nile flows north into the Mediterranean Sea.

CHAPTER 2

Pharaohs and Everyday People

Egyptians called their rulers kings, queens, or pharaohs. Whatever their title, they were the most important people in ancient Egypt. They made the laws and were in charge of the army.

This is a statue, or stone carving, of a pharaoh.

Believe it or not, the Egyptian people had things that we would find in our own homes today. This ancient Egyptian queen is playing a board game.

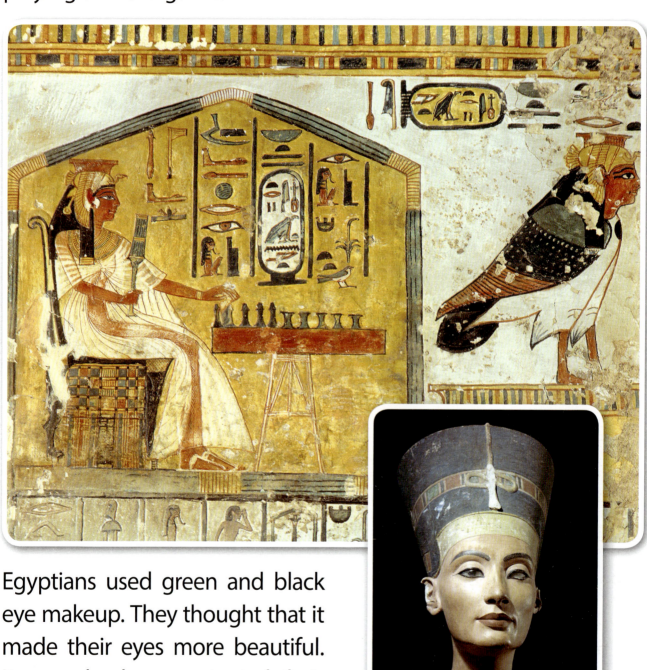

Egyptians used green and black eye makeup. They thought that it made their eyes more beautiful. It may also have protected their eyes from the sun—and kept away little flies.

Egyptian workers made bricks from mud and straw. The bricks were used for building. The bricks were dried in the hot sun until they were hard and strong.

Egyptians traveled by boat on the Nile River. The boats were also used to carry food from one part of the kingdom to another.

CHAPTER 3

Pyramids and Mummies

In ancient Egypt, pyramids and tombs were burial places for important people, such as pharaohs. Pyramids were made from stone blocks.

It took thousands of people and millions of stone blocks to build a pyramid. After the stone blocks were cut, they were pushed and pulled on sleds across the sand by workers.

When important ancient Egyptians such as pharaohs died, their bodies were treated in a special way. For example, everything inside a pharaoh's body, except the heart, was taken out. The pharaoh's insides were placed in canopic jars.

The rest of the body was then wrapped in lots of strips of cloth and placed in a wooden box. The wrapped body is called a mummy. Often, a painted mask was placed over the mummy's face.

Are you wondering what happened to the pharaoh's heart? Ancient Egyptians believed that their gods and goddesses would judge every pharaoh's life by weighing the pharaoh's heart. If a pharaoh had been good, he would have a light heart. But if he had not been good, his heart would be heavy. Here a god is weighing a heart.

When a pharaoh's body was ready, it was taken to a tomb or pyramid. The walls of these burial places were painted with pictures of things the pharaohs enjoyed when they were alive.

Many treasures made of gold and jewels have been found buried inside Egyptian tombs and pyramids. The mummies of Egyptian pharaohs have been found too. Here you can see part of a necklace.

This gold lion's head was part of a pharaoh's bed. Can you imagine? Pharaohs had solid gold decorations on their beds!

Gods and Goddesses

Here you can see some Egyptian gods and goddesses with human bodies and animal heads. The gods are shown this way because ancient Egyptians believed in animal gods too. They also believed the gods and goddesses made good and bad things happen in the world.

The Sphinx of ancient Egypt is a huge statue in the desert. It has a human head and an animal body. Can you see that it has the body of a lion? The Sphinx was a symbol of a god and a pharaoh.

Three of the most powerful Egyptian gods are shown here. The god Osiris has a green face. His wife, Isis, is next to him. Horus, their son, has the head of a falcon.

Egyptians believed that Horus's eye protected the living and the dead. His eye was often drawn on the walls of tombs.

The god Anubis has the face of a jackal. A jackal is a wild dog. Egyptians thought that the gods and goddesses were clever and smart like certain animals.

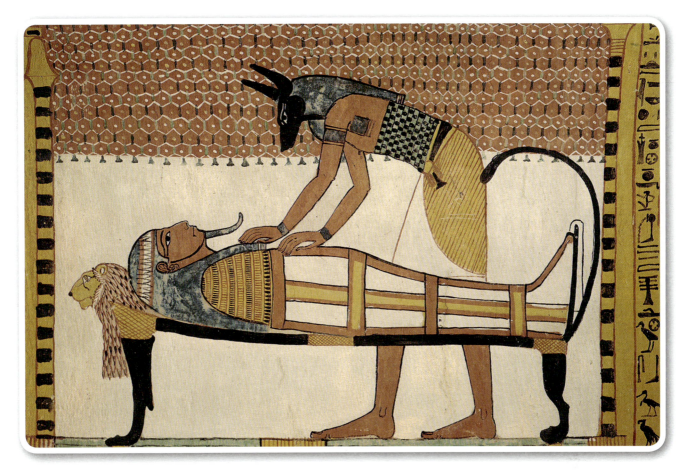

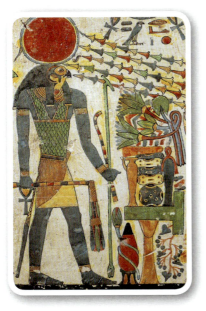

The Egyptians' main god was Re, the sun god. He is always shown with the sun above his head. The goddess Ma'at is usually shown wearing an ostrich feather.

CHAPTER 5
Egyptian Writing

Ancient Egyptians used little pictures, called hieroglyphs, to make words. The hieroglyphs shown here were carved on a stone wall.

Egyptians also wrote on paper, which they made from the papyrus plant. Sometimes the sheets of paper were joined together to make scrolls.

In ancient Egypt, scribes knew how to read and write. They wrote important information on walls and on paper. This Egyptian man is a scribe.

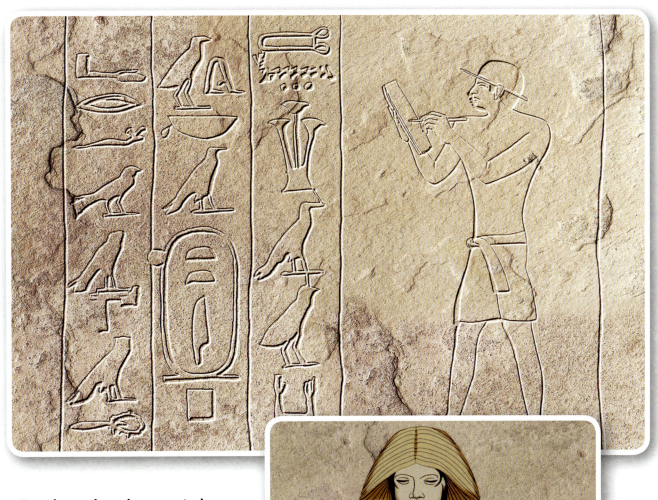

Scribes had special tools, including writing boards made of wood. These boards were like little desks that could be carried around.

Hieroglyphs look like pictures. Each picture could be a sound, part of a word, or a whole word. These beautiful hieroglyphs reveal the name of a king.

CHAPTER 6

Tutankhamen

For thousands of years, people hoping to become rich have tried to find the pharaohs' tombs and treasures. Howard Carter and Lord Carnarvon were two such men. After much searching, and to their great delight, they found King Tut's tomb.

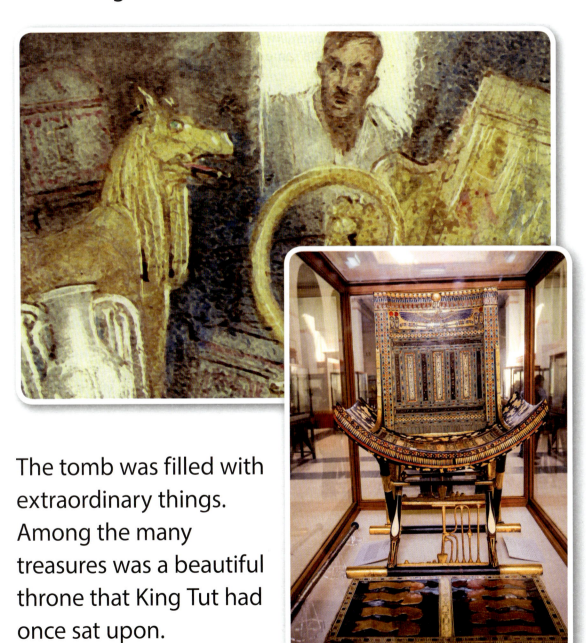

The tomb was filled with extraordinary things. Among the many treasures was a beautiful throne that King Tut had once sat upon.

Incredibly, they found King Tut's mummy! The mummy had been inside the tomb for thousands of years.

On the mummy, there was a golden mask of King Tut's face. Before long, the whole world heard about these exciting discoveries.

This sculpture, also found inside the tomb, shows the face of the young King Tut. Like many important Egyptians, his head was shaved so that he could wear a wig. Egyptians also wore wigs so that itchy bugs couldn't get into their hair!

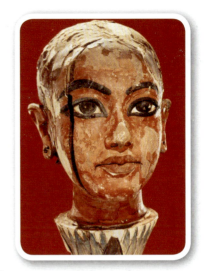

This chariot belonged to King Tut. It is possible the young King Tut rode into battle or through the streets of an Egyptian city on this chariot.

This box, found in King Tut's tomb, was made to hold jewelry. There are hieroglyphs all over the box.

This is the Rosetta Stone. The words on the stone helped people understand ancient Egyptian writing. Because of the Rosetta Stone, we have learned about pharaohs and gods, the games Egyptians played, and the food they liked to eat!

CHAPTER 7

Hatshepsut

Another very famous pharaoh was Hatshepsut. Hatshepsut became a pharaoh after her husband died. She had to work very hard to show that a woman could be a pharaoh too!

Hatshepsut was a great pharaoh. She sent Egyptians on an ocean voyage to get the things that were needed back home in Egypt. This ocean voyage happened about 3,500 years ago.

The Egyptians brought back sweet-smelling oils, gold, ivory, plants, and valuable wood. Hatshepsut was very pleased to see these things.

CKHG™
Core Knowledge History and Geography™

Editorial Directors
Linda Bevilacqua and Rosie McCormick

Subject Matter Expert

Nadine Brundrett, Department of Classics, Brock University

Illustration and Photo Credits

3LH/SuperStock: 21

A detail of a wall painting in the tomb of Rekhmire showing women playing the harp, lute and tambourine / Werner Forman Archive / Bridgeman Images: 11

Age fotostock/SuperStock: 9

Ancient Egypt, Wall painting, The eye of Horus, Tomb of Sennedjem, Thebes, Deir el Medina, 19th dynasty (photo) / Photo © Mary Jelliffe / Bridgeman Images: 14

Anubis attends Sennedjem's Mummy, from the Tomb of Sennedjem, The Workers' Village, New Kingdom (mural) (see also 67892), Egyptian 19th Dynasty (c.1292-1187 BC) / Deir el-Medina, Thebes, Egypt / Bridgeman Images: 15

Coffer from the treasury of the tomb of Tutankhamun (c.1370-52 BC) New Kingdom (wood & ivory with applied gold & silver), Egyptian 18th Dynasty (c.1567-1320 BC) / Egyptian National Museum, Cairo, Egypt / Bridgeman Images: 22

DeAgostini/SuperStock: 15

Deceased making libations in honour of Gods, scene from Book of Dead, funerary papyrus, Egyptian civilization, 3rd Intermediate Period, 19th Dynasty / Egyptian National Museum, Cairo, Egypt / De Agostini Picture Library / W. Buss / Bridgeman Images: 13

Egypt, Ancient Thebes, Shaykh 'Abd al-Qurnah, mural of farmers at work / De Agostini Picture Library / G. Dagli Orti / Bridgeman Images: 3

Egypt, Karnak, Red chapel of Hatshepsut, relief of wine offering to Hatshepsut / De Agostini Picture Library / Bridgeman Images: 16

Egyptian art. Great Temple of Ramses II. Colossal statues depicting the pharaoh Ramses II (1290-1224 BC. Abu Simbel. Egypt. / Tarker / Bridgeman Images: 5

Harrison Neil/Prisma/SuperStock: 12

Howard Carter (1873-1939) English Egyptologist near golden sarcophagus of Tutankhamon (mummy) in Egypt in 1922 (photo Harry Burton) colourized document / PVDE / Bridgeman Images: 20

Howard Carter discovered the lost burial chamber of Tutankhamen (colour litho), Watt, John Millar (1895-1975) / Private Collection / © Look and Learn / Bridgeman Images: 19

Iberfoto/SuperStock: 24

Investigation on the grave treasures of Tutankhamen (b/w photo) / © SZ Photo / Scherl / Bridgeman Images: 20

Isis and Horus honouring Osiris shown as mummiform, Sarcophagus detail, Egyptian civilization / Egyptian National Museum, Cairo, Egypt / De Agostini Picture Library / W. Buss / Bridgeman Images: 14

Jed Henry: 3

Joduma/Pixabay: 16

Metal processing and brick making, detail from frescoes in Tomb of Rekhmire, Sheikh Abd el Qurnah Necropolis, Luxor, Thebes (Unesco World Heritage List, 1979), Egypt, Egyptian civilization, New Kingdom, Dynasty XVIII / De Agostini Picture Library / S. Vannini / Bridgeman Images: 7

Mummy in coffin, from Hawara (mixed media), Egyptian Ptolemaic Period (332-30 BC) / Ashmolean Museum, University of Oxford, UK / Bridgeman Images: 9

Nefertari playing senet, detail of a wall painting from the Tomb of Queen Nefertari, New Kingdom (fresco), Egyptian 19th Dynasty (c.1292-1187 BC) / Valley of the Queens, Thebes, Egypt / Bridgeman Images: 6

Pectoral decorated with the winged scarab protected by Isis and Nephthys, from the tomb of Tutankhamun (c.1370-52 BC) New Kingdom (gold cloisonne and glass paste), Egyptian 18th Dynasty (c.1567-1320 BC) / Egyptian National Museum, Cairo, Egypt / Bridgeman Images: 12

Peter Barritt/SuperStock: 23

Queen Hatshepsut receiving offerings, 2009 (colour litho), Baptista, Fernando G. (21st century) / National Geographic Image Collection / Bridgeman Images: 24

Scala/SuperStock: Cover B, 15

Shari Darley Griffiths: i, iii, 2, 7, 8a, 8b, 13

The cartouche of the king, from the Tomb of Horemheb (1323-1295 BC) New Kingdom (wall painting), Egyptian 18th Dynasty (c.1567-1320 BC) / Valley of the Kings, Thebes, Egypt / Bridgeman Images: 18

The crowned head of Nefertiti, wife of Akhenaton / Werner Forman Archive / Bridgeman Images: Cover A, 6

The gold mask, from the Treasure of Tutankhamun (c.1370-52 BC) c.1340 BC (gold), Egyptian 18th Dynasty (c.1567-1320 BC) / Egyptian National Museum, Cairo, Egypt / Bridgeman Images: Cover C, 20

The Rosetta Stone, from Fort St. Julien, El-Rashid (Rosetta) 196 BC (see also 138897), Egyptian Ptolemaic Period (332-30 BC) / British Museum, London, UK / Bridgeman Images: 22

The Weighing of the Heart against the Feather of Truth, from the Book of the Dead of the Scribe Ani, c.1250 BC (painted papyrus), Egyptian 19th Dynasty (c.1292-1187 BC) / British Museum, London, UK / Bridgeman Images: 10

Treasure of Tutankhamen, royal chariot from New Kingdom / De Agostini Picture Library / S. Vannini / Bridgeman Images: 21

View on the Nile, 1855 (oil on canvas), Seddon, Thomas (1821-56) / Ashmolean Museum, University of Oxford, UK / Bridgeman Images: Cover D, 4

Wael Hamdan/age fotostock/SuperStock: 19

Workers dragging building blocks (papyrus), Egyptian 21st Dynasty (c.1069-945 BC) / Private Collection / Ancient Art and Architecture Collection Ltd. / Bridgeman Images: 16